Diaries *of* POETRY

SHERRY KIDD

authorHOUSE®

AuthorHouse™
1663 Liberty Drive
Bloomington, IN 47403
www.authorhouse.com
Phone: 833-262-8899

Published by AuthorHouse 08/04/2020

ISBN: 978-1-7283-6861-0 (sc)
ISBN: 978-1-7283-6983-9 (e)

Print information available on the last page.

Any people depicted in stock imagery provided by Getty Images are models, and such images are being used for illustrative purposes only. Certain stock imagery © Getty Images.

This book is printed on acid-free paper.

Because of the dynamic nature of the Internet, any web addresses or links contained in this book may have changed since publication and may no longer be valid. The views expressed in this work are solely those of the author and do not necessarily reflect the views of the publisher, and the publisher hereby disclaims any responsibility for them.

A Beautiful God

Oh what a beautiful God

Beautiful blue oceans and streets paved with the purest gold and the saints standing in heaven with their long beautiful white robes covered in the blood of Jesus

I look afar there sits my mind a million miles away in the depths of eternity to where a beautiful God will be

Touching his spirit is like looking through his eyes and seeing his awesome glory the splendor of all his ways a beautiful God is all that I can see

A Beautiful God

Treasure Chest

There opens the door there sits the treasure chest not a mere vessels of wood and metal and when you find the key and unlock the treasure chest there sits a golden pillow not just a pillow but what is in the midst of the pillow is the great treasure our hearts and from our hearts to your heart which is more valuable than diamonds, rubies, and fancy cars and we will treasure you in our hearts forever more which will last forever and ever

Treasure Chest

Seasons

What is Seasons

Seasons is a time set for God blessing

Seasons is being overcome with tiny drops of rain to give you a broad spectrum of changes in life

Seasons is uplifting your spirit and your spirit connect with your heart to gratify your soul to reach your vision

Seasons is to speak your blessing into existence and to tarry your feet to walk through crack glass that tears your heart into pieces to mend your broken heart into gladness that exceeds your expectations

Seasons

Voices

What is Voices

Voices is carousing through beams of light that travels to a massive mountains of hope

Voices is suppressing our thoughts of anxieties that carry us to the depths of overflowing seas to the bottom of secret treasures

Voices is carrying our voices to silver brooks initiating our white picket fences to our glory of destination unknown

Voices is a ideas that carries us to the highest prize that makes us recognize our tendencies that trap our deficiencies that bound us to our realities

That is Voices

Empty

What is Empty

Empty is nothing in you but air that suffocate your spirit

Empty is there is no life in you nobody to revive you helpless to your inner self wishing to leave but cannot

Empty is longing for love there is no one to love you beyond your emptiness

Empty there is nothing in there but air losing its voice to express your character that leads your lifeless body to resuscitate to a breaking point out of this century

That is Empty

Brown Sugar

Brown Sugar is your countenance is silky brown that glows in the illumination of the light where darkness cannot dwell

Brown Sugar is breaking down the barrier between dark skin and light skin that separate us that is causing division between our heritage

Brown Sugar is being what you dream always conquering what is in God's thought of you

Brown Sugar is being who God taught you to be not what you wanna be never ceasing to exist beyond your existence

Brown Sugar

Sherry Kidd

Great

Great is to have the power over your circumstances

Great is to empower yourself to create a powerful outlook on life and erase all the sins that keep you bound

Great is to withdraw yourself from all the poison that contaminate your being not to make you pass your breaking point

Great is reaching a desired outcome that caresses your bones to navigate points of light to a never ending behavior to balance your passion

That is Great

Tears

What is Tears

Tears is drop of water falling down from your eyes that carry your soul to dimension unknown

Tears create bridges of waterfalls that flows from oceans of hope

Tears carry your heart to deep daydreams of compassion for your fellowman

Tears is crying my last tear that represent a season of gratitude that helps me get pass all my insecurities that linger through mountains of faith

Tears

Here

What is Here

Here is where I stand and the power within me that transcend into a supernatural force that reckons a beautiful picture

Here is being there in a holistic sphere that carries a movement of things in the past life

Here is creating your essence in a massive portion of a earthquake that shake the very essence of our being

Here is tearing down the gates of hell to rise above the fire and brimstone of judgment that bring you to your peak

Here

Lovin Yourself

Lovin yourself is lovin yourself when nobody else will

Lovin yourself is lovin yourself in your own spirit and accomplishing your dreams and desires to prosper and be who you are

Lovin yourself is finding what captures your heart to love what fails to exist

Lovin yourself is lovin yourself beyond the borders of heaven that reflect your inner being that accept the promises you made to yourself

Lovin yourself

I Wish

I Wish is following your dreams to the highest level that leads you into your destiny

I Wish is not letting people talk you out of your desires that make you successful

I Wish is wishing upon a star that take you to another dimension of the unknown

I Wish is being who you are in your own skin never letting go of your positive vibe that promises to be undeniable

I Wish

You

What is you

You is painting a picture that reveal God's heart that captures a shooting star from the sky that makes you feel beautiful

You is never ceasing to be who you are but to carry each thought to your destination that will render your expectation to a deeper level

You is seeing the silver crooked lines that carries the waves to the echoes in the sky that reveals the angels on a ladder that reaches to the heaven ascending and descending your blessings coming down like miniature drops of rain touching your soul

You

Believe

What is Believe

Believe is never stop believing in yourself and conquering your demons that try to possess your dreams

Believe is going toward the crossroads of your destiny that bring you into your own power that releases you into the air that you breathe

Believe

Blackness

Blackness is being proud of your blackness and not being ashamed of who you are

Blackness is your skin is black mocha that shine through the bright light that creates a glow to never cease to exist beyound its creativity

Blackness is every race looking toward your magnificent power to rule your words that make a person take precedent over your own mind

Blackness

Open

Open is to open your heart to receive your dreams that overcome you

Open you cannot see what is inside of you that makes you want to reveal your inner thoughts that confine you to your destiny

Open is to face your fears face to face with substituting your courage for faith that make you believe in you self

Open

Silver Bells

Silver Bells is when you die and hear the silver bells ringing and see God presence and he say enter into my joy

Silver Bells is when a multitude of holy angels is singing praises to God and the silver bells ringing for eternity

Silver Bells is when you see all of your family and friends ringing the silver bells to capture your spirit in your heavenly body and when you see the saints dress in white ringing their silver bells

Silver Bells is when Jesus take you by the hand and take you through the pearly gates and you go to the top of the mountains of glory and seat you with God

That is Silver Bells

Friends

What is Friends

Friends is someone who will be there in the end

Friends never let you down always around to pick up the pieces

Friends is someone who keep their promises never break their oath and always keep coming to your rescue

Friends is someone who will fight for you even in the midst of losing their dignity never being caught up in quarrelsome behavior that require no effort

That is my friend Starr Child

A Beautiful Spirit

A Beautiful Spirit is a sweet spirit that longs for God's touch embracing the beauty within

A Beautiful Spirit is a beautiful swan that floats on a ocean that whisper in the ears of create on that marvelous sweet noise in the clear blue sky

A Beautiful Spirit is reckoning the secret mysteries of the past and future

A Beautiful Spirit is total dependence on God that enables a spirit to continue living truth that has no lies in it

A Beautiful Spirit

Victory

Victory is winning over the enemy

Victory is turning yesterday losses into tomorrow victories that turn into trophies that remind us of our decisions to conquer our defeats

Victory is lifting our consciousness to revive our lifeless body to breathe air into our lungs without gasping for our last breath

Victory is fearing nothing man can do but lifting ourselves in victory that leads us to rebuking all of our past memories of despair that cut us like a spinning blade

Victory

Black Beauty

Black Beauty is millions of stallion of black horses rushing through the mighty wind sound like the power of an earthquake

Black Beauty is circles of light of blackness that illuminates the space to carry black beauty to the earth's atmosphere

Black Beauty is zillions of promises up before God's throne to carry black beauty to the area of the perimeters that measure the whole heaven

Black Beauty is the bond of unity that rise together to bring you in the limelight of the forest that limit our desire to isolate our being

That is Black Beauty

I AM

I AM free to live life the way I was born to be

I AM free from my mind completely to leave you and never come back to your trail of deception that binds my spirit

I AM free to be happy to find my true love that will never cast me away into eternity

I AM

Courage

What is Courage

Courage is not letting fear overtake you and being the best you can be

Courage is getting up the nerve to do what you couldn't do when you were afraid

Courage is fighting those evil spirits that try to possess your inner being

Courage is telling yourself that you can make it no matter how hard your flesh try to stop you from being the person God made you to be

That's Courage

Sherry Kidd

Life

Life is what you make it out to be

Life is to believe your heart and you mind believe your soul that is a anchor for your transparency to help you learn from your mistakes

Life do not stop moving for reality it is reality

Life is seasons of moments that conquer our revelations to seek out our demons that gives you no rest

God IS

What is God IS

God IS the Father, Son, and the Holy Spirit

God IS my compassionate heart that makes me have love for mankind

God IS never failing to make ends meet for me and my family and resting in his presence

God IS my life he never lets me down he always picks me up to carry on with life everlasting that is reaching toward a never ending Glory!

God IS

Sherry Kidd

Write

Write is writing a book about my life story

Write is writing on a wing and prayer desolate to our thinking negative thoughts

Write is to bear our resilience of our character that weaken our flesh to descinerate into the air

Write is to stand for righteousness that let our heart beat fearlessly to continue our relentless motivation to move a nation to stand together

Write

My First Love

First Love is your eyes meet and your heart beats fast this is the man you thought you would love for a lifetime

First love is he brings you a dozen of long stem red roses showing you he loves you because he cannot live without you

First love is cherishing all the memories that you had together that brings you into a mountain of hope that never leave you alone not even for a second

First love is loving him beyound his faults and walking to the pathway of matrimony to capture the essence of our first time we fell in love never forgetting the moment

Sherry Kidd

Love

What is Love

Love is having affection for one another there is no hate in love

Love is not hurting the one that you are with just being a friend

Love is never connecting with a man that has no love for you just moving on to the man that loves you

Love is gentle, peaceful, and giving

Love is what you make it out to be in your mind love carries a multitude of compassion that lifts the spirit of a man that makes him love you more

That is Love

A Broken Spirit

A Broken Spirit is being broken into many pieces that gives your heart no rest

A Broken Spirit is to cease to find hope that challenges you to be the best that you can be in life

A Broken Spirit gives no strength to your mind it break you down to powder never carries you to your destiny

A Broken Spirit is never being able to settle in your mind what is making you broken never trusting your ideas to conquer your emotions to evaporate your pores into deep thoughts

I Sing

I Sing is singing to the Glory of God what is in your heart that flows to your mind

I Sing is to sing in loud voices that captures the existence of many angels that sings with you

I Sing is watching out for amazing melodies that brings the puzzle together to fit perfectly in the empty space that carries to a wonderful place of unexpected solitude

I Sing

What If

What If I could turn back to see where life would take me

What If I could look through the hourglass and see a vision of my life passing me by

What If I could paint a cloud in the sky and see God's hand wiping away my tears

What If

Sherry Kidd

Joy

What is Joy

Joy is breathing with air like walking on the waves of the ocean that brings happiness beyound your dreams

Joy is a source of gratitude that engages in pure excellence that brings every thought into subjection

Joy is breaking down your sadness and to carry your seed of gladness to a deeper level

Joy is to bring into captivity the little drops of pain that hurts you it eliminates all of your fears and leaves you with nothing but joy

There

What is There

There I stand wishing my mind would stand and take notice to calculate all the mistakes I made

There I will fly to the innermost parts of the world and capture all the tears of people born before you

There is a beautiful bouquet of roses that fills the room with the sweetest smell you ever tasted

There

Sherry Kidd

Someday

Someday I am gonna finish what I started and never look back on the past

Someday I am gonna reach my hands into the sky and bring down all my blessings

Someday I am gonna make someone less fortunate than me reach their goal

Someday mountains move faith and moves hills to captures valleys that move your victories to win wars that causes you to conquer your enemies that try to consume your life

Someday

I Miss You

I Miss You God you are inside my spirit I cannot live without you there by my side

I Miss You because you are my breath when I cannot breathe

I Miss You there is no hope but your revealed will tells me to never give up

I Miss You because I am longing for your touch of your embrace to cause me to enter in your charismatic spirit that never fails to exist

I Miss You

Sherry Kidd

I Think

I Think bigger than I dream

I Think is being surrounded by a beckon of light that illuminates my countenance to be all that I am

I Think is caressing by my invisiable parts to enter in my mind into my heart to manipulate my pupils to see inside of our facial expressions

I Think of attributes that lead me into my destiny that carry me to a place to point me in the right direction to think of eternity that will exist beyound a lifetime

I Know

I Know is millions of empty promises disappearing into the atmosphere seeking to release time when it first begun

I Know is staying outside to capture a flowing sphere that made aspirating incapable of swallowing your own vomit that makes you able not to see what is so clear

I Know is entering the black hole never to return from the place where you started from to experience real trouble that never seeks to blind your faults

I Know

Sherry Kidd

Echoes

Echoes is hearing the sound in your ears that travel to your mouth that beat like a drum the echoes in your voice

Echoes is building your house on sandcastles that make you think of your childhood memories of your mother's words that make a reiterating sound that make echoes in your mind remember her attributes the melodies of her heart

Echoes is never ending to cease from reality but always tearing down walls of despair that conquer your demons to echo your goodness that make you desert all of your fears

Echoes is to carry your burdens to be out of this dimension that rather be a sounding brass that carry our dreams and desires to a place unknown to the human kind

Echoes

Peace

What is Peace

Peace is to have a clear mind that you would not even utter the things you could not see

Peace is flowing like a river that gives you the shivers

Peace is hearing the voice of God that tells you to be quiet in the midst of noise

Peace is flying high above the blue skies that bring rain that pours down droplets of love that carries your peace into the heavenly realms

Peace is like soft classical music that plays each note to perfection it drowns out every offense that makes peace amazingly unique

That is Peace

Faith

Faith is believing in something you cannot see that has not arrive yet

Faith is believing in God that never let us down he makes a way for us

Faith is never stop believing in our dreams that makes us live life knowing that it going to happen to us no matter how hard we try to fail

Faith

One God

One God that is mightier than all creation

One God that makes us realize our differences in such a awesome way

One God that lifts me up in my spirit to never give up to always have faith in him

One God that never seeks darkness but always seek light that moves a person to be who they are I and the mirror

One God

Printed in the United States
By Bookmasters